Meditation Handbook

By

Emerson D. Brooking, Ph.D.

Emerson D. Brooking, Ph.D.

Panther Brook Spiritual Center

P.O. Box 55

1000 Panther Brook Lane

Turnerville, Georgia 30580

emerson@pantherbrook.com
www.pantherbrook.com

©2016 Emerson Dean Brooking, Ph.D.

ISBN-13: 978-0692749210
(Panther Brook Spiritual Center)

ISBN-10: 0692749217

Publisher: Panther Brook Spiritual Center

Publication Date: September 8, 2016

Contents

Meditation Handbook

Benefits of Meditation

Roy Eugene Davis states that regularly meditating to a level of superconsciousness allows the innate purity of your essence of being to purify your mind and illumine your consciousness. Such meditation results in the following benefits:

1. **Physical Benefits**: Stress reduction; relief from stress-related symptoms; slowing of biological aging processes; enhanced immune function; refinement of brain centers through which spiritual qualities can be more easily processed.

2. **Psychological Benefits**: Increased ability to focus, concentrate, and think more rationally; increased ability to let go of distracting thoughts; increased peace of mind; respite from relentless mind-chatter; weakening of addictive tendencies, harmful habits, and troublesome subconscious conditionings.

3. **Spiritual Benefits**: Experience of wholeness; increased compassion; clearing of outmoded thought patterns; increased intuition, insight, and creativity; increased ability to view events and circumstances with dispassionate objectivity; enlightenment (identification as Self instead of self).

(Above Section Used with Permission)

Meditation Handbook Summary

Meditation is a **relaxed, focused, uninterrupted awareness**. In this book, I present sufficient information for you to begin or deepen your meditation/prayer practice. As I briefly describe the information to be presented, each term that is bold, italicized, and underlined can be found in the Table of Contents and on the page indicated.

RELAXED AWARENESS

Meditation requires the ability to let go and let God. If you are unable to relax, deep meditation is unlikely.

Probably the easiest way to relax is to focus on belly breathing. The _**Diaphragmatic Breathing Exercise**_ (p. 6) is a good introduction. If you are a chest breather and have difficulty breathing into your belly, lie in _**The Crocodile Posture**_ (p. 8). This posture will teach you the appropriate muscles to use to breathe diaphragmatically.

When you are a proficient belly breather, then master Three Part Breathing (_Deergha Swaasam_) described by Swami Satchidananda in his article _**The Breath of Life**_ (p. 9). When done correctly, you will actually be breathing in seven times more air than you usually inhale in a normal breath. Other useful relaxation techniques are described in _**"Mini" Relaxation Exercises**_ (p. 13).

The _**Introduction to Progressive Muscle Relaxation**_ (p. 15) and _**Progressive Muscle Relaxation Instructions**_ (p. 15) will provide you with a powerful entry into deep relaxation. Just remember to keep breathing full, deep breaths as you tighten and release the major muscle groups in your body.

During and at the end of your progressive muscle relaxation, do not forget to include some autogenic suggestions. _**Introduction**_ *to Autogenic Training* (p. 18) and *Autogenic Training Instructions* (p. 19) will outline the procedure.

To help you understand more deeply how powerful deep relaxation (*yoga nidra*) and meditation can be, study the *Koshas* (p. 20).

When you feel like you are totally relaxed and could not possibly relax any further, take your finger temperature. If it is not 95°s or higher, raise it. The autogenic suggestion, "My hand is warm and heavy" may help. Or take your GSR2 unit and lower the tone. See *Thermal Biofeedback* (p.22) and *Electrodermal Biofeedback* (p. 24).

Begin your meditation/prayer practice with *Alternate Nostril Breathing Instructions* (*Naadi Suddhi*, Nerve Purification, p.25). [If your nose is congested, do a *Neti (Nasal) Wash* (p. 28) first.] Remember to do your Three Part Breathing (*Deergha Swaasam*) throughout your Alternate Nostril Breathing exercise.

FOCUSED AWARENESS

In this book, I outline several techniques to help focus and relax your mind. Teaching meditation to a lot of people over many years has taught me that, if you are open to practicing various meditation techniques, you will eventually find one that suits you well. There are many from which to choose.

However, the trick is to not jump around too fast, using lots of different techniques. You must use each one long enough to truly experience it. If practiced daily, a month may be sufficient for you to make that judgment. This is part of the art of discovering a useful meditation technique.

My "hook" into meditation practice was the Serenity Meditation. *Introduction to Serenity Meditation* (p. 29) and *Serenity Meditation Instructions* (p. 30) describe the technique.

Mindfulness (Vipassana) Meditation Instructions (p. 33) are written quite clearly and include someone you can contact if you have any questions.

Kriya Pranayama Meditation is a simple, but powerful, meditation technique. It is best taught by personal transmission. You should have a teacher (guru) personally initiate you in this practice. If you wish more information, contact Roy Eugene Davis at www.csa-davis.org

Mantra meditation is another meditation technique. *Behavioral Medicine Applications* (p. 36), *The Relaxation Response* (p. 37), *Learning to Elicit the Relaxation Response* (p. 39), *Relaxation Response Instructions* (p. 41), *Focus Word or Phrase* (p. 43), and *Common Focus Word or Phrases* (p. 44), describe the technique well.

Introduction to Christian Centering Prayer (p. 45) and *The Method of Christian Centering Prayer* (p. 47) describe another possibility.

Other meditation techniques include listening to the inner sound and/or contemplating the inner light. *Caffeine* (p. 53) and *Technique of Primordial Sound and Light Contemplation* (p. 54) describe how you can develop the ability to hear the inner sound and/or see the inner light.

UNINTERRUPTED AWARENESS

To be successful in meditation/prayer usually requires consistent effort, determination, and practice over a long period of time. It also requires you to develop a strong moral foundation. *Yoga Philosophy* (p. 57), *Integral Yoga*® (p. 59), and *Raja Yoga: The Yoga of Meditation* (p. 60) expound this truth.

Until you live a virtuous life, success in meditation/prayer is doubtful. How does one who covets, lies, cheats, steals, kills, and/or engages in sexual misconduct quiet the mind? That mind will always be agitated!

If you do not develop a strong moral foundation, you may learn powerful meditation techniques, but your life and consciousness will not be transformed. You will never harvest the fruits of the spirit – a loving, compassionate heart filled with peace and joy.

RELAXED AWARENESS

Breath

Diaphragmatic Breathing Exercise

By A. Martin Wuttke

PURPOSE & BENEFITS:

The purpose of this exercise is to make you very conscious of your breathing patterns. By consciously regulating your breathing pattern and breathing in a manner that reflects deep relaxation, you interrupt the cycle of stress and, at the same time, release accumulated stress and tension from your mind and body.

WHEN TO PRACTICE:

Four times a day, 5-10 minutes each practice session.
Ideally:
1. Before getting out of bed in AM.
2. Before lunch.
3. Before dinner.
4. After you are in bed, before you go to sleep.

HOW TO PRACTICE:

1. Get as comfortable as possible – relax your muscles.

2. Take three complete, deep, cleansing breaths.

3. Breathe diaphragmatically: Concentrate on your abdomen – between your navel and the lower part of your sternum. (Place your hand there if you are having difficulty.)

4. Breathe only moving your abdomen: As you inhale, your abdomen should expand and rise slightly; as you exhale, your

abdomen should contract. Keep your shoulders and the rest of your body completely still.

5. (a) For general relaxation: Make the length of inhalation the same as the length of exhalation. (If you inhale to the count of three, exhale to the count of three.)

5. (b) For insomnia, hyper arousal and panic symptoms (NOT FOR DEPRESSION): Make your exhalation twice the length of your inhalation. (If you inhale to the count of three, exhale to the count of six.)

6. Breathe only through your nose – make your breath smooth, rhythmic, gentle, and silent – with as little effort as possible.

7. If thoughts intrude, just keep returning your attention back to your breath.

8. Continue for 5-10 minutes.

(Above Section Used with Permission)

Experience has taught me that, if you can learn to breathe diaphragmatically, it will solve many anxiety issues. During my career, several students have cited diaphragmatic breathing, belly breathing, as the **most important skill** they have **learned!!!**

Many report having gained hours of additional sleep. They wake up in the middle of the night and, instead of staying awake, they focus on slow belly breathing and soon fall back asleep.

During the day, if they become anxious, they focus on slow belly breathing and the anxiety diminishes. In fact, research has shown that it is impossible to have an anxiety attack while belly breathing.

To have an anxiety attack, you must be chest breathing. Rapid chest breathing can actually <u>cause</u> an anxiety attack! Therefore, if you want to stop an anxiety attack, move your breathing from the chest to the diaphragm, to your belly.

The Crocodile Posture

As infants, one hundred percent of us start out life as diaphragmatic breathers. Unfortunately, as we age, eighty percent of us shift to chest breathing. Chest breathing is very inefficient breathing, chronically depriving us of the vital oxygen we need for good health.

This shallow breathing creates a chronic stress response, increasing our blood pressure, heart rate, muscle tension, etc. It also decreases alpha and theta brain wave activity – brain waves associated with relaxation. This chronic stress response also increases the likelihood of developing addictions.

Regrettably, many of us no longer know how to use the muscles needed for diaphragmatic breathing. The staff of the Himalayan Institute in Honesdale, Pennsylvania emphasizes the usefulness of the Crocodile Posture in teaching the correct muscles to use in breathing.

The Crocodile Posture is accomplished by lying on the stomach, legs about hip-width apart and toes pointing in or out. Fold your arms and place your hands on the opposite elbows, drawing elbows in toward body so that the shoulders and upper chest are off the floor.

Resting your forehead on your arms, close your eyes and relax. This posture locks the chest muscles so you are forced to breathe diaphragmatically, thus teaching you the correct muscles to use while breathing.

The Himalayan Institute staff also recommends using a sandbag to help strengthen the muscles used in diaphragmatic breathing. The instructions are to lie on the back, place the bag over the lower belly, and practice making the bag rise on the in-breath.

The Breath of Life

By Sri Swami Satchidananda

Prana: The Vital Force When you breathe, in addition to the oxygen, you also take in a lot of prana. The oxygen gets diffused in the lungs and then gets into the bloodstream, but the prana goes throughout the body. It enters into every area – physical, vital and mental. Every cell of your body vibrates with new life.

Prana is our very life. It is the vital force that pervades the entire cosmos. You get prana from food, from the sun and from the air you breathe. You can live for many weeks without food, days without water, minutes without air, but not even for a fraction of a second without prana.

In Sanskrit, if you deify the prana you can call it *Parashakti*, the Cosmic Power. Wherever you see power, you see the action of prana. Even the movements in an atom are due to the prana within it. The light and heat in a flame are prana. Electricity is prana. Your motorcar moves with prana – gasoline is a liquid form of prana. To raise your hand you need prana. Your breathing is prana. Your digestion is prana. Even to think you need prana, because it is the subtle prana that moves the mind.

All movement everywhere is caused by prana, the cosmic energy. The entire nature is moving constantly. That is the nature of the nature – constant movement and transformation. And it is the prana that causes all the movement. So why should we want to control it?

Pranayama: Controlling the Cosmic Power In pranayama we are trying to handle and control the cosmic Shakti. Pranayama is composed of two words: "prana" and "ayama." "Ayama" means regulation, control, or mastery. We begin by regulating the prana that moves our own bodies and minds.

When we gain mastery over the prana, we have mastery over the inner nature, too, because it is the prana that creates all the movements in an individual – physical and mental. We try to control the inner nature, because it is the nature's movement that causes a lot of disturbance in the system and makes it impossible for the Light within to shine in its true, original way.

When we can control the prana inside, we can control the prana outside, too. They are one and the same force on different levels. The body is a microcosm, and the universe outside is a macrocosm. So, by the regular practice of pranayama, we are able not only to control and direct the prana that functions within us, but the universal prana as well.

Yogic Breathing With proper pranayama you begin to use the entire lungs. You take in much more than your normal quota of oxygen and prana. It can be measured in laboratory tests.

In normal breath, you inhale five hundred cubic centimeters of air, and then you breathe out the same. After your exhalation, the lungs are almost empty. Still, there is residual air in the lungs. After you breathe out your normal five hundred cubic centimeters, if you pull your tummy in slightly, you can exhale some more air, which has been measured as sixteen hundred cubic centimeters.

Now you begin to inhale. You first inhale the air that you squeezed out – sixteen hundred cubic centimeters. Then you inhale your normal five hundred. And then afterwards, you can inhale some additional air. If you inhale more deeply, you can take in another sixteen hundred cubic centimeters. So, after a complete squeezing out on the exhalation, you can inhale thirty-seven hundred cubic centimeters.

So, instead of your usual five hundred cubic centimeters, you can take in thirty-seven hundred cubic centimeters – more than seven times as much as in a normal breath. In every breath you can take in seven times more air, more oxygen, and more prana if you do the pranayama regularly.

Imagine the advantage. The quality of the blood improves and the richness of the blood is the basis of the entire body's health. Your blood gets more oxygenated. Oxygen is life. It is a great panacea, a fine medicine for all kinds of poisons. When you have that much vitality, no virus can even think of coming near you. As soon as it comes near you, burn it out. That is the beauty of pranayama.

Benefits of Pranayama The main purposes of pranayama are to purify the system and to calm and regulate the mind. Pranayama purifies the nervous system and eliminates toxins from the body and blood.

It helps in the curing of asthma, consumption, and other respiratory disorders. With proper breathing, you can eliminate the excess mucous which causes most hay fever and sinus discomfort. You can exhilarate the blood circulation and stimulate the entire body quickly. Pranayama produces lightness of body, alertness of mind, good appetite, proper digestion, and sound sleep.

Pranayama helps you to attain radiant health, but that is only a secondary benefit, a by-product, of the practice of pranayama. The main aim is to control the mind through the prana. If you can control the mind, you are the master. The prana – here as the movement of the breath – and the movement of the mind – go together.

If you regulate the prana, you have regulated, through the movement of the breath, that same pranic movement in the mind. Should you ever feel upset, tense, or worried, do some slow deep breathing with full attention on the breath, and you will easily bring the mind to a calm state.

According to the *Yoga Sutras*, a veil of mental darkness covers the Light within. The benefit of pranayama is that it removes this veil, and the mind becomes clear and fit for concentration. So, pranayama is a beautiful preparation for meditation. Before meditation, do three rounds of Bastrika, the bellows breath. It will exhilarate the entire body, drive off drowsiness, remove tension, and bring harmonious movement in all the cells.

After this, do some alternate nostril breathing, or some slow, deep breathing through both nostrils at the same time. Follow the breath with the mind. Feel how it comes in, how far it goes, and how it returns. Calm, slow, and steady breathing will also keep the mind very calm.

To derive the maximum benefit, go slowly in developing your practice. Be patient. Pranayama should never be done in a hurry, nor should you try to advance too quickly, because you are dealing with vital energy.

The Yoga scriptures personify prana as a deadly cobra. So, remember you are playing with a cobra. If you play well and make the cobra dance, you will accrue many benefits, as did the snake charmers in India. They used their snakes for their livelihood. But if they didn't play properly, they would be killed. In the same way, with prana, you should be very careful. Do everything gently; avoid even the slightest strain, and never hurry.

(Above Section Used with Permission)

When you are a proficient belly breather, then master Three Part Breathing (*Deergha Swaasam*) described by Swami Satchidananda. The instructions are simple:

Breathe in to the belly, then the chest, and finally the upper chest, so even your collar bones rise. Then breathe out in just the opposite manner, emptying the upper chest, the chest, and the belly. Draw in the belly at the end of the out breath to exhale all the air. And then begin again. Do not hold the breath at any point and do not strain. Breathe only through the nose.

Over the years, my students have consistently reported that one of the most beneficial lessons they have learned in my classes is pranayama, breath control. It is a technique they can use every day, wherever they are.

Those, who wake up during the night, successfully use it to go back to sleep, thus often gaining hours of additional sleep. Others use it throughout the day to help maintain balance, to be more peaceful and joyful. Experience has taught me not to underestimate the value of pranayama!

"Mini" Relaxation Exercises

By Benson-Henry Institute for Mind Body Medicine

Mini relaxation exercises are focused breathing techniques which help reduce anxiety and tension immediately!

You can do them with your eyes open or closed (but make sure that your eyes are open when you are driving!).

You can do them any place, at any time; no one will know that you are doing them.

Ways to "Do a Mini"

Switch over to diaphragmatic breathing; if you are having trouble, try breathing in through your nose and out through your mouth, or take a deep breath. You should feel your stomach rising about an inch as you breathe in, and falling about an inch as you breathe out. If this is still difficult for you, lie on your back or on your stomach. You will be more aware of your breathing pattern.

Remember, it is impossible to breathe diaphragmatically if you are holding your stomach in! So... relax your stomach muscles.

Mini Version 1

Count very slowly to yourself from ten down to zero – one number for each breath. Thus, with the first diaphragmatic breath, you say "ten" to yourself; with the next breath, you say "nine," etc. If you start feeling light-headed or dizzy, slow down the counting. When you get to "zero," see how you are feeling. If you are feeling better, great! If not, try doing it again.

Mini Version 2

As you inhale, count very slowly up to four; as you exhale, count slowly back down to one. Thus, as you inhale, you say to yourself "one, two, three, four;" as you exhale, you say to yourself "four, three, two, one." Do this several times.

Mini Version 3

After each inhalation, pause for a few seconds; after you exhale, pause again for a few seconds. Do this for several breaths.

Good times to "Do a Mini"

While being stuck in traffic ... when put on "hold" during an important phone call ... while waiting in your doctor's waiting room ... when someone says something which bothers you ... at all red lights ... when waiting for a phone call ... in the dentist's chair ... when you feel overwhelmed by what you need to accomplish in the near future ... while standing in line ... when in pain ... etc., etc.

THE ONLY TIME THAT MINIS DO NOT WORK IS WHEN YOU FORGET TO DO THEM!!! So go "Do a Mini!" ... .

(Worksheet, from *The Wellness Book: The Comprehensive Guide to Maintaining Health and Treating Stress-related Illness,* courtesy of the Benson-Henry Institute for Mind Body Medicine, www.bensonhenryinstitute.org)

Progressive Muscle Relaxation

Introduction to Progressive Muscle Relaxation

I understand meditation to be a "relaxed, focused, uninterrupted awareness." The ability to relax is, therefore, essential for a productive meditation practice. If the meditator is unable to "let go and let God," little progress will occur.

When I later learned about yoga, I discovered that one approach to *yoga nidra* (deep relaxation) was progressive muscle relaxation. The following is a progressive muscle relaxation routine.

In yoga, one starts relaxing at the feet and moves up the body to the top of the head. This mirrors yoga's emphasis on encouraging an upward flow of *kundalini,* a flow of energy from the base of the spine to the top of the head.

Progressive Muscle Relaxation Instructions

Progressive muscle relaxation involves learning to tense and release muscle groups throughout the body. The objective is to become more aware of the distinction between tension states and relaxation states, thus providing you with self-control procedures designed to reduce unnecessary anxiety and tension. With practice you will learn to induce total bodily relaxation.

Progressive muscle relaxation is best learned in a quiet setting and in a prone position. Tense each muscle group for five to seven seconds. Then release tension immediately rather than gradually. For thirty to forty seconds, enjoy the feelings in the muscles as they loosen up, smooth out, unwind, and relax more and more deeply.

Do one or two tension/release cycles per muscular group, concentrating on the differences between tension and relaxation. Once a muscle group is relaxed, do not move it unnecessarily.

A.   Legs and Feet (start with dominant side first, then non-dominant side)
      1. Push toes toward back wall
      2. Pull toes toward head
      3. Keeping leg straight, clinch thighs and raise legs and feet a few inches off supporting surface

When you relax, do not slowly lower your leg, nor should you slam it down. Rather, let it fall like a ripe fruit falls from a tree. Just release it. It is as though your leg is supported by a string, and someone cuts the string and the leg drops.

Very slowly and mindfully, move your foot back and forth, finding a comfortable position, and forget about it. (This "forgetting about it" is an important step to learn. Deep meditation cannot easily occur unless all sense doors have been closed.)

Now do the same procedure for the non-dominant hand and arm

B. Buttocks, anus muscles, pelvic area
      1. Tighten your buttocks, anus muscles, pelvic area

C. Belly
      1. Breathing in through the nostrils, fill up the belly with air. Like blowing up a balloon, blow it up even higher.
      2. Open your mouth and let the air gush out! (This is not a quiet out breath.) Imagine all the tension in the body gushing out with the breath.

D. Chest
      1. Breathing in through the nostrils, fill up your chest with air
      2. Open your mouth and let the air gush out! (Once again, this is not a quiet out breath.) Imagine all the tension in the body gushing out with the breath.

E. Shoulders
      1. Lift your shoulders and try to touch your ears

2. Push your shoulders in front of the chest, like you want to touch your shoulders together in front of the chest
3. Push your shoulders down toward your feet, like you want to touch your feet

F. Hands and Arms (start with dominant side)
    1. Splay out your fingers
    2. Make a fist
    3. Keeping your fist, lift your arm and hand a few inches, keeping your arm straight
    4. Relax
    5. Now slowly roll your hand back and forth, find a comfortable position, and forget about it

G. Neck
    1. Lift head just an inch or two and tighten all muscles in neck by pushing chin toward chest, but keeping it from touching chest
    2. Relax
    3. Now very slowly roll head back and forth. Find a comfortable position and forget about it.

H. Face
    1. Bite hard and pull back corners of mouth
    2. Open mouth, move jaw up and down and all around
    3. Stick out tongue as far as you can
    4. Squint eyes and wrinkle nose
    5. Lift eyebrows toward forehead
    6. Take all the muscles of face and try to touch your nose

After each of the muscle groups has physically been tensed and relaxed once or twice, mentally scan each muscle group throughout your body and let go of any remaining tension. This can be accomplished by breathing in – focusing, and breathing out – relaxing. As you breathe in, you focus on the tension in that area of the body. As you breathe out, you allow that tension to flow out with your out breath.

Now, as you become totally aware of the good feelings of relaxation, warmth, and calmness throughout your body, silently repeat to yourself a sacred word or phrase. With practice you will learn to associate your sacred word or phrase with feelings of calmness and relaxation.

Whenever you find yourself becoming tense or anxious, think of your sacred word or phrase. As you silently repeat it to yourself, feel calmness and relaxation sweeping over your body. When you are relaxed, it is easier to maintain inner balance and stability, and to deal fully and clearly with every situation you face. It also allows you to move more deeply into your meditation practice.

Like all skills, learning to relax takes practice. If you practice relaxing, you will get better at relaxing. It is best to practice with the whole body supported.

Autogenic Training

Introduction to Autogenic Training

For several years, I discussed autogenic training in my Stress Management classes. During each course, I led my students in autogenic training exercises.

Over the years I have learned to appreciate the power of autogenic training. Having introduced hundreds of students to autogenics, I never cease to be amazed at some of their responses. Autogenic-induced states sometimes allow deeply repressed memories to surface in a most vivid, intense fashion.

During autogenic training, several of my students have had flashbacks to prior experiences of sexual and physical abuse. I believe that any relaxation exercise can potentially produce these flashbacks. However, my experiences indicate that autogenic training, as a form of self-hypnosis, is a more powerful technique than most of the others.

It should, therefore, be approached with some care. Although particularly unpleasant "autogenic discharges" must be managed with clinical skill and sophistication, they are not to be avoided. Indeed, they indicate the power and usefulness of autogenic training.

Autogenic Training Instructions

Autogenic training is probably the world's most widely used self-regulation therapy. The term "autogenic" is derived from the Greek words *autos*, meaning self, and *genos*, meaning origin. Therefore, in this structured self-hypnosis technique, the self-regulation and self-healing powers of the mind are channeled in a positive manner, repeating phrases in a state of passive concentration.

Sit or lie in a physically relaxing position, allowing all thoughts and distractions to pass without judgments. Watch thoughts passively, as if you had entered a movie theatre and your thoughts were being shown on a movie screen in front of you, or you were riding in a car and your thoughts were like billboards passing on the highway.

While you concentrate on body sensations in a passive manner, without directly or volitionally bringing about any change, mentally repeat the following six standard phrases:

1. My (choose dominant arm) is very heavy. (Repeat four to six times.)
2. My (choose dominant arm) is very warm. (Repeat four to six times.)
3. My heartbeat is calm and regular. (Repeat four to six times.)
4. It breathes me. (Repeat four to six times.)
5. My solar plexus is warm. (Repeat four to six times.)
6. My forehead is cool. (Repeat four to six times.)

Periodically, while repeating the six standard phrases, you should occasionally repeat one or more of the following positive intentions:

I am calm.
I am relaxed.
I am quiet.

If deep relaxation is not achieved immediately, you may rest assured that it will come later, with more practice.

When you successfully achieve an autogenic state, it should not be abruptly terminated. Rather, you should slowly reactivate muscular and breathing systems. This is achieved by wiggling the fingers and toes, breathing in deeply a few times, and, finally, opening the eyes.

Please note that blood vessel dilation and associative relaxation have a particularly tranquilizing and sleep inducing effect. However, blood vessel dilation is not harmless, since the changed distribution of blood influences the entire organism. Therefore, autogenic training should only be instituted by healthy individuals for whom no vascular risks are known to exist.

Koshas (Deep Relaxation and Meditation)

Koshas

From Satchidananda Ashram

(There are five sheaths to us, covering the Atman or true self, which is unchanging and eternal.)

ANAMAYA KOSHA – PHYSICAL SHEATH
Has six expressions: Existence, Birth, Growth, Modification, Decay, and Death.
It is a tool to enhance awareness.

PRANAMAYA KOSHA – VITAL ENERGY SHEATH
Contains prana or vital energy of self. Can be controlled with the breath. It is the link between body and mind, and we can use it to control the mind. This is the level of the aura, chakras and nadis (meridians).

MANOMAYA KOSHA – MENTAL SHEATH
Consists of perceptual organization, habits, language, and emotions. It is connected to the senses. Fears and desires are part of the Manomaya Kosha, also acting impulsively.

VIJNANAMAYA KOSHA – INTELLECTUAL SHEATH
Discrimination, the ability to discern. The witness. Critical thinking, cause/effect relations.

Sometimes a battle between the Manomaya Kosha and the Vijnanamaya Kosha. "I know I shouldn't, but I want to." (from fears and desires).

ANANDAMAYA KOSHA – BLISS SHEATH
Experience of inner harmony and peace. Intuition.
Absolute self-confidence; equanimity, sense of well-being.
Balanced mind leads to Anandamaya Kosha

ATMAN – TRUE SELF
One with all. The True Witness.
The Pranamaya through Anandamaya Koshas compose the human soul. They continue on after the body dies and eventually take another birth.

(Above Section Used with Permission)

If one can truly "let go" during *yoga nidra* (deep relaxation) and meditation, consciousness, "the witness", will move from *Anamaya Kosha* (Physical Sheath) to Pranamaya *Kosha* (Vital Energy Sheath) to *Manomaya Kosha* (Mental Sheath) to *Vijnanamaya Kosha* (Intellectual Sheath) and rest in

Anandamaya Kosha (Bliss Sheath). This is why *yoga nidra* (deep relaxation) and meditation are so powerful.

It can be extremely disconcerting to be suddenly disturbed while resting in *Anandamaya Kosha,* while resting in Bliss. The person can be thrown into confusion and lose all composure. For this reason, care and sufficient time should be taken when ending *yoga nidra* (deep relaxation) and meditation.

Biofeedback

Thermal Biofeedback

Biofeedback is a means to discover internal processes. The concept that there is a direct link between finger temperature and cortical activity is particularly useful.

You probably already have a thermometer sitting around your home somewhere. If you do, go find it. If you do not, go buy one. It can be quite inexpensive and will provide you useful information about how stressed you are and the effectiveness of your relaxation strategies.

Hold the tip of your thermometer (thermistor) with your thumb and index finger. You may instead wish to tape the thermistor to the index finger. If you do use tape, be sure not to wrap the tape all the way around your finger, as that would restrict blood flow to the finger. Just use enough tape to attach the thermistor.

Once you know your finger temperature, try to increase it by increasing the blood flow to your hand. Use the relaxation skills you already have or try some you are learning in this book. Generally, as finger temperature increases, alpha and theta brain wave activity (which is associated with relaxation) also increases.

Finger Temperature
70°- 80° = high stress
80°- 85° = moderate stress
85°- 90° = stressed
90°- 95° = good
95°- up = excellent

With some exceptions, finger temperature is a good judge of a person's stress level. Cardiac patients often have finger temperature in the low 70's. They are usually chronic chest breathers, denying their bodies sufficient oxygen.

When cardiac patients learn to raise their finger temperature to the low 80's, they often report being more relaxed than they have ever been. Without thermal biofeedback, they might never learn how much more relaxed they could become. That is the usefulness of biofeedback! It tells us what is actually happening in our bodies.

The clinical goal is a finger temperature of 95 degrees. (It is more difficult to move finger temperature from the 80's to the 90's than from the 70's to the 80's.)

Please keep in mind that, from a meditation/prayer standpoint, being totally relaxed is very helpful. Remember that the definition of meditation is "a relaxed, focused, uninterrupted awareness." The ability to relax, to let go, is key to success in meditation.

Of course, there are some confounding variables that must be considered when using thermal biofeedback. If the room is too cold or too hot, finger temperature may not be valid.

Some people are "thermal responders," that is, their fingers are always warm, no matter how stressed they are. Other people have circulation problems and their hands are always cold. For these reasons, I also recommend that you use a GSR (Electrodermal) biofeedback device. It will not have thermal biofeedback's confounding variables.

Electrodermal Biofeedback

Electrodermal biofeedback [aka skin conductance or galvanic skin response (GSR) biofeedback] is more difficult to manipulate than thermal biofeedback. Because it is so difficult to manipulate and artificially control, it is one of the modalities utilized in a lie detector test.

Since electrodermal biofeedback is more difficult, it is often used after one has achieved mastery of thermal biofeedback. Raising your finger temperature is easier than increasing the electrical conductance of your skin.

Several years ago I purchased thirty-five GSR2 units from Thought Technology and, during the following years, used them with a variety of populations – pre-school, middle and high school, college students, cardiac patients, alcohol and drug addicts, participants in relaxation and stress management workshops, and individual clients. Once, I carried the device for an entire day and learned much about what caused me stress and what relaxed me.

The GSR2 precisely monitors your stress levels by translating tiny tension-related changes in skin pores into a rising or falling tone. By resting two fingers on the sensing plates you learn to lower the pitch and your stress level. You basically get "biological" feedback through the GSR2 as you learn to relax and as you get better at doing it, you'll find yourself relaxing faster with or without the GSR2.

(Quoted from www.thoughttechnology.com
Above Paragraph Used with Permission)

If you do not already have access to a GSR device, I recommend you purchase Thought Technology's "GSR2 Biofeedback Relaxation System." It holds up well and is a useful learning tool.

The current price is around $75 and includes the biofeedback unit, earphone, instructional CD (Side 1: "How to get the most from your GSR2", Side 2: "fully-narrated relaxation exercise"), 9V battery and operator's manual. If you mention this book, *Meditation Handbook,* you will receive a 10% discount. To order, go to www.thoughttechnology.com

Alternate Nostril Breathing

Alternate Nostril Breathing Instructions

By A. Martin Wuttke

PURPOSE & BENEFITS:

The following technique produces a state of sympathetic/parasympathetic balance. It will also cause brainwave patterns to become more synchronized. The result will be a more settled, calm, and centered state of being.

WHEN TO PRACTICE:

Alternate nostril breathing can either be performed by itself or as a preparation for any other type of relaxation exercise. (It is most beneficial before meditation.)

HOW TO PRACTICE:

1. Sit up straight... feet flat on the floor... spine, neck and head in alignment. Let your left hand rest on your left thigh, palm facing up... eyes closed.

2. Bring your right hand up so that your palm is in front of your face. You will be using your thumb to close the right nostril and your ring finger and little finger together to close the left nostril. Curl your index and middle finger into the palm of your hand and just let them relax.

3. Take a deep inhalation ... close the right nostril with your thumb and exhale through the left nostril ... inhale through the left nostril ... close left nostril with your ring and little finger ... release thumb and exhale through right nostril ... inhale through right nostril ... (That completes one cycle.) ... close right nostril with your thumb . . . release ring and little finger and exhale through left nostril.

EXAMPLE:
Exhale left
Inhale left
Exhale right
Inhale right
(These four make one full cycle.)
Exhale left, etc.

4.   Your breath should flow quietly in a smooth even rhythm without any pauses, breaks, or jerkiness. Your inhalation and exhalation should be even in length.

5. Begin with five full cycles of alternate nostril breathing. When the exercise becomes effortless and smooth, you can go as high as twelve cycles.

(Above Section Used with Permission)

Alternate nostril breathing is a useful prelude to your meditation/prayer time. By balancing the two hemispheres of the brain, positive conditions are created for deep meditations. When you have mastered the technique, begin to make the exhalations longer than the inhalations, eventually twice as long.

But remember to **never strain** while doing any of the breathing exercises.   If you find yourself gasping for air, back off immediately! Just relax and breathe normally. With practice, you will eventually develop better breath control and experience its benefits.

Focus on eventually having the exhalation twice as long as the inhalation. If you breathe in to the count of three, breathe out to the count of six. You can gain more control over your breath by using *Ujjayi* Breathing.

In *Ujjayi* Breathing you constrict your throat, slightly closing the glottis, like you were trying to fog a mirror. *U*jjayi Breathing makes a slight sound and gives you more control over your inhalation and exhalation.

But always remember, when doing pranayamas, not to strain. Back off if you find yourself gasping for air. Because you are dealing with such delicate organs as the lungs, heart, and the nerve centers, take great care not to strain.

Pranayamas are so powerful that many yoga teachers never teach them in beginning classes. <u>So act responsibly</u>!

In this book, I am not giving instructions on *Kapalabhati* (Skull Shining), *Bhastrika* (Bellows Breath), breath retention, or *Bandhas* (locks). I feel it is wiser and safer to learn these skills while directly supervised by a teacher (guru).

Neti (Nasal) Wash

If your nose is blocked and you cannot practice alternate nostril breathing, try clearing your nostrils by performing a neti (nasal) wash. A neti wash involves pouring warm saline solution through one nostril and then the other.

I once had an opportunity to discuss with John Clarke, M.D., the Medical Director of the Himalayan Institute, my difficulty in doing a neti wash (nasal wash). Years earlier I had tried doing a daily neti wash because Roy Eugene Davis recommended it.

Almost immediately, I got an ear ache. Throughout my life, I always had problems with ear aches and I feared nasal washes would lead to them. So I decided I would never be able to successfully do nasal washes because I could not tilt my head while pouring water in my nostril without the procedure later causing ear aches.

Dr. Clarke drew a picture of the human head on the board. He insisted that, even if I held my head upright, I could pour water into one nostril and it would come out the other without entering the ear canal.

With this encouragement, I returned home and began a daily nasal wash. I found that Dr. Clarke was correct and I encountered no problems. I have continued to do nasal washes twice daily, and am sure my health has improved because of it.

In yoga, breathing freely through both nostrils is said to aid in harmonizing the active and passive systems of the body, and therefore the neti wash is a helpful practice before meditation. Alternate nostril breathing, a powerful pranayama, is very difficult to do well if the nose is congested.

Neti wash (nasal wash) containers can be easily purchased in most nationwide chain stores, near the pharmacy area. They are not expensive. If you can buy a porcelain neti pot, it can be easily cleaned and lasts a long time. If you buy a large container of salt, make sure it pure salt and contains no additives, especially iodine.

When you fill your neti pot with warm, clean water, use approximately one-quarter teaspoon of salt. If you experience discomfort while doing your nasal wash, vary the water temperature and/or amount of salt. Neti wash should never be uncomfortable!

FOCUSED AWARENESS

Serenity Meditation

Introduction to Serenity Meditation

I called this meditation technique the "Serenity Meditation" because its use often left me feeling tranquil and serene. A month of daily practice should allow you to decide if this meditation technique is useful for you. Experience teaches me that the Serenity Meditation can be useful for all people, irrespective of their religious beliefs or lack thereof.

The following is my summary of the Serenity Meditation. If anyone practicing this technique has questions, please feel free to contact me.

Serenity Meditation Instructions

Imagine a round crystal (or, if you prefer, a small cross) which is very clear, warm, and bright, and which has brilliant light waves emanating from it. As you direct the path of the crystal around and through your body, feel it illuminating and cleansing both your mind and your body, leaving you with a profound sense of tranquility. All movement of the crystal should be very slow and deliberate. All circles are clockwise.

The mind is like a caged drunken monkey, stung by a scorpion, dashing and darting about from one thought to another. Concentration on the crystal acts as a "brake" on the mind and empties the mind of other thoughts. In addition, the crystal illuminates and cleanses both mind and body.

Path of crystal is as follows:

1. Start at your umbilicus (navel) and circle 9 times.

2. Move up to your xiphoid [xiphisternum – the small extension of the lower part of the sternum (chest bone) between the ribs] and circle 3 times.

3. Do figure eights around your breasts 3 times.

4. Move up to the sternal notch (jugular notch, right below Adam's apple) and circle 3 times.

5. Move up to your Adams apple and circle 3 times.

6. Move up to your lips and trace their outline 3 times.

7. Move up to your nostrils and trace each nostril opening 3 times, beginning with the right nostril.

8. Move up to your eyes and trace the outline of each eye 3 times, beginning with the right eye.

9. Move up to just above the junction of your eyebrow lines. Circle 3 times, imagining bright red streaks of fire moving from the crystal into the head.

10. Move up to the center of forehead, just below hair line, and circle 3 times. Imagine rays of white light illuminating your brain.

11. Move to the top of head and circle 9 times.

12. Move to occiput (back of head) and circle 3 times.

13. Move down spine to base of spine, directly opposite navel, and circle 3 times.

14. Circle waistline 3 times.

15. Begin moving up from waist on right side of body. Move up to right armpit, down inside of arm, over middle finger, up outside of arm, over shoulder to right ear. Circle right ear 3 times.

16. Move up to top of head and circle 3 times.

17. Move to left ear and circle 3 times.

18. Move over left shoulder, down outside of left arm, over middle finger, up inside of arm to armpit, down left side of body to waist.

19. INJECTION PROCESS – Imagine injecting a cord through the center of your body, starting on your left side at your waist and moving to your right side. Then imagine injecting a second cord through the center of your body, starting at the navel to your spine.

20. Move crystal up to your nostril. As crystal enters nostril, silently repeat your sacred word or phrase 3 times.
Males: Crystal enters right nostril.
Females: Crystal enters left nostril.

Move crystal inside skull to spot just above junction of eyebrow lines. This is the same position outlined in step #9 except now crystal is inside of body. Once again imagine bright red streaks of fire emanating from the crystal.

21. Imagine the crystal descending through the center of your body, coming to rest at intersection of the two cords, previously mentally created, running perpendicular to each other. This resting point is in the center of your body, a distance of two fingers above your navel. The crystal continues to emanate light rays in all directions.

The crystal remains here during meditation. (When I practiced, I found it useful to move the crystal back up to the position outlined in #20. This position is sometimes called the "third eye" or "Christ Center.")

22. The crystal then moves up through the center of your body and exits through your nostril.
Males: Crystal exits left nostril.
Females: Crystal exits right nostril.

Buddhist Concepts Because I wanted the Serenity Meditation to appeal to a wide audience, I stripped the technique of its Buddhist concepts. However, there may be some Buddhists (and others) who will want to know what these concepts are.

In Thailand, where I first learned it, it was called Buddhanusati, "Buddho," meditation. Some of the Buddhist concepts include the following:

1. Nine circles – eight times represent the Eightfold Path (Right Understanding, Right Thought, Right Speech, Right Action, Right Means of Livelihood, Right Endeavor, Right Mind Control, and Right Meditation), and the ninth Nirvana.

2. Three circles – once for the Buddha, once for the Dharma (law), and once for the Sangha (order of monks).

3. As the crystal enters the nostril, silently repeat "Buddho, Buddho, Buddho."

Mindfulness (Vipassana) Meditation

Mindfulness (Vipassana) Meditation Instructions

Vipassana Meditation is a powerful practice, opening areas within me I did not know existed. When I did not have an extended period of time to practice, I would do the Serenity

Meditation. When I had a longer period of time, I would do vipassana meditation, both sitting and walking.

Meditation Exercises to Cultivate Presence

(Adapted from a summary by Robert Wootton, Ph.D. and used with his permission. Robert has offered to answer any questions you may have. He may be contacted at rw.home@frontier.com)

Two Principles:

(1) There is just what there is. Our task is to know (by direct feeling, not thinking about it) what each moment's experience is. When one sits, stands, or walks, know that there is sitting, standing, or walking. When there is sensation in the body, whether pleasant, unpleasant, or neutral, know that there is pleasant, unpleasant, or neutral sensation.

When one sees something, know that there is seeing. When thoughts or visual images appear, know that there is thinking or seeing, without getting lost in the content, story line, or meaning of the thought or vision. When sounds call attention, know that at that moment there is hearing; and, if thoughts or feelings occur about the sound, know that at that moment there is thinking or feeling.

(2) Only the mind that clings to nothing, and is able to both open to and let go of everything, can be fully present and know what there is in each moment. Thus, when a sensation arises, one is willing to experience it as it actually is for as long as it lasts and to let go of it when it changes or ceases.

Let go of ideas about how meditation should be and acknowledge what is actually occurring. This direct, non-judgmental contact with experience allows and is a transformation of our normal compulsive manner.

Two Occasions for Practice:

(1) **Sitting**:   Focus attention on the sensations of breathing wherever it occurs most predominantly, either at the nostrils or in the chest-abdomen area. Allow breathing to occur and change however it will. Feel the sensations of the in-breath or the rising movement, and the sensations of the out-breath or falling movement, however long or short, soft or tense, rhythmic or irregular it may be. Be with the entire duration of each in and out or rise and fall, noticing the beginning and ending moments.

To help maintain focus, make soft mental notes: "in," "out," or "rising," "falling." If sounds, sensations, or thoughts call attention away, experience these with equal attention and note "hearing," "feeling," or "thinking."   As soon as sounds, sensations, or thoughts recede, gently return to the sensation of breathing.

If there is discomfort and an impulse to move, notice the feelings and the intention. Then move slowly enough to notice the sensations of moving. If drowsiness or nodding occurs, focus attention on those sensations. Do the same for other mental states such as boredom, agitation, etc.

Maintain attention on the sensation of breathing as the predominant object of awareness. At whatever point one notices the attention elsewhere, note what is occurring and return to the breath. There is no need for judgment or criticism; but, if they occur, note them also. Do the same for controlling the breathing.

(2) **Walking**: Pick a short space in which to walk back and forth. Walk at a slow enough pace to move one foot at a time and distinguish the three parts – lifting, moving, placing.

Focus attention on the sensations of each part, however one experiences each in the body.   To aid focus, note "lifting," "moving," "placing." The technique is then the same as for sitting. Try to feel directly and in minute detail exactly what the experience of walking and breathing is.

The aim is to cultivate the kind of continuous, accurate mindfulness that would allow one to give a summary afterwards of the changing sensations and objects of consciousness that occurred.

Mantra Meditation

Behavioral Medicine Applications

In Cape Cod, Massachusetts, I attended training in Behavioral Medicine Applications. It was taught by Herbert Benson, M.D., and others in his program.

Herbert Benson's use of the term "relaxation response" really appealed to me. It was a neutral term, a Western, science-based concept that was easily accepted by the people with whom I was working. Learning about the relaxation response simplified my presentations to groups representing a variety of religious affiliations.

Many of the conservative, fundamentalist, Southern Appalachian folks got <u>very</u> nervous when I talked of meditation, mantra meditation, etc. Hearing talk of "eliciting the relaxation response by using a focus word or phrase" was much more acceptable to them.   Generally, unless individuals are comfortable with the terms and concepts presented, they are unlikely to practice and learn relaxation skills.

The following are copies of some of the handouts I received during training. I have used them often in my work and have found them quite helpful:

The Relaxation Response

The mind/body model of health suggests that our modern world – with its stresses, strains, and incessant changes – causes or aggravates many of our symptoms. You cannot always change your environment, and in many cases may not want to. But what can you do about the stresses of modern life? One answer lies within you.

By learning to use your awareness and your mind, you can begin to control your physical reactions to stress. You can cultivate the ability to turn within to give yourself a respite – a chance to slow down, relieve tension and anxiety, and renew yourself. First let us examine the physiology of stress.

The *Fight-or-Flight* Response The *fight-or-flight response,* also called the stress response, was first identified by Dr. Walter B. Cannon of the Harvard Medical School early in this century. It is a profound set of involuntary physiological changes that occur whenever we are faced with a stressful or threatening situation. This response, critical to the survival of primitive humankind, prepares the body for a physical reaction to a real threat – to fight or flee.

Today, however, we do not often face the life threatening situations that primitive people responded to frequently, and the fight-or-flight response cannot distinguish between a serious threat and the everyday stresses of modern life. In fact, simply recalling a threatening or frightening situation is often enough to trigger the fight-or-flight response.

The fight-or-flight response is an integrated reaction controlled by the hypothalamus, an area of the brain. Confronted by a threat – physical or emotional, real or imagined – the hypothalamus causes the sympathetic nervous system to release epinephrine and norepinephrine (also called adrenaline and noradrenaline) and other related hormones. When rapidly released into the body, these powerful messengers propel you into a state of arousal. Your metabolism, heart rate, blood pressure, breathing rate, and muscle tension all increase.

Recently, researchers studying the long-term effects of the fight-or-flight response have concluded that it may lead to permanent, harmful physiological changes. The fight-or-flight response is useful and, in fact, necessary in times of emergency. But the stressors of modern living elicit it at times when it is inappropriate for us to run or fight.

We must find ways to control the harmful aspects of this primitive physiological response and so neutralize the negative effects of modern stress on our health and well-being. The relaxation response can do just that.

A Counterbalancing Relaxation Response As demonstrated by researchers around the world and suggested by age-old wisdom, there is a *counterbalancing mechanism* to the fight-or-flight response. Just as stimulating an area of the hypothalamus can cause the stress response, so reducing the stimulation results in relaxation. The relaxation response is an inborn set of physiological changes that offset those of the fight-or-flight response. These changes are coordinated; they occur together in an integrated fashion.

The physiological changes of the fight-or-flight response and the relaxation response are polar opposites. In the fight-or-flight response, metabolism, heart rate, blood pressure, and muscle tension all **increase**. In the relaxation response, metabolism, heart rate, blood pressure, and muscle tension all **decrease**.

If the stresses of modern life cause the fight-or-flight response, the relaxation response can be used to counteract the harmful effects of stress. Just as the heart begins to beat rapidly when you imagine a frightening situation, your mind can be used to slow your heart rate.

There is one other significant difference between the fight-or-flight response and the relaxation response – the fight-or-flight response usually occurs involuntarily, whereas conscious elicitation of the relaxation response most often needs to be practiced.

[Worksheet adapted from *The Wellness Book: The Comprehensive Guide to Maintaining Health and Treating Stress-related Illness* (pp. 33-38), courtesy of Benson-Henry Institute for Mind Body Medicine, www.bensonhenryinstitute.org]

Learning to Elicit the Relaxation Response

The relaxation response is a state of profound rest that can have lasting effects throughout the day if you practice it regularly. What is relaxation? Many of us use the image of "letting go."

Physically, we mean releasing muscles from habitual, unconscious tension. We try to breathe more slowly and regularly, letting go of tension with each outbreath. Emotionally, we mean cultivating an attitude of greater equanimity. Mentally, we mean observing and letting go of troubling, worrisome thoughts. All of us can experience an enhanced ability to relax as we practice these different approaches to letting go.

Many people have difficulty relaxing their bodies: you think you are relaxed, when, in fact, your neck muscles are still tense. Cultivating a state of quiet acceptance in a world that demands so much is a new experience for many of us.

To use an automotive image, shifting down from overdrive can be difficult for those accustomed to the fast lane. Yet, to restore a healthy balance, your body and mind need exactly such a change in pace.

To elicit the physiological state called the relaxation response, you need to develop techniques that help you "let go" more deeply than most of us can without such help. Remember that the relaxation response is a physiological response inborn to everyone, and it can occur at times when you are not even aware of it.

Bring to mind, for example, a time when you were lying on the beach on a warm summer day or moments at night when you drift into sleep. In both instances, the relaxation response is believed to account for the pleasant state and its measurable physiological changes. You can develop your innate ability to use these techniques in the most beneficial ways possible.

The relaxation response can be elicited by a number of techniques that involve mental focusing. All of these techniques have two basic components: the first is the *repetition* of a word, sound, phrase, prayer, image, or physical activity; the second is the *passive disregard of everyday thoughts* when they occur during relaxation.

As you try the different methods of eliciting the relaxation response, you may find that one method works better than others or that one or two of the techniques prove to be the most helpful. Or you may choose to make a combination of all the techniques part of your personal health regimen.

Find your own balance. Bear in mind that the goals of eliciting the relaxation response are straightforward, practical, and potentially transformative. Those who practice eliciting the relaxation response commonly report these kinds of changes:

- decrease in stress-related physical symptoms
- decrease in anxiety
- freedom from compulsive worrying, self-criticism
- increase in concentration and awareness

- improved sleep
- greater self-acceptance
- enhanced performance and efficiency

Spirituality Research studies confirm that such changes can occur with regular elicitation of the relaxation response. In addition, a recent study of the relationship between spirituality and health conducted by Jard Kass, Ph.D., and colleagues at Boston's Deaconess Hospital, found that a significant number of those who regularly elicit the relaxation response, regardless of method, reported an increase in positive attitudes associated with spirituality.

Spirituality in this study was linked to increased life purpose and satisfaction. They also found that increases in positive attitudes contributed to improvements in health. Regular elicitation of the relaxation response cultivated health-promoting attitudes which decreased the frequency of medical symptoms.

People who regularly elicit the relaxation response generally begin to describe themselves as more peaceful, energetic, self-accepting, happier, and so forth. Less preoccupied with past and future, they learn to enjoy the present moment more fully. In short, whatever their cultural or spiritual tradition, people can enjoy the benefits of the relaxation response in whatever way is most appropriate for them.

[Worksheet adapted from *The Wellness Book: The Comprehensive Guide to Maintaining Health and Treating Stress-related Illness* (pp. 33-38), courtesy of Benson-Henry Institute for Mind Body Medicine, www.bensonhenryinstitute.org]

Relaxation Response Instructions

1. Sit in a comfortable place but try not to lie down. If you lie down on your bed, chances are you will fall asleep. You may sit in a chair, on the floor with a cushion against the wall, or on the

bed with a pillow behind you. If you must lie down, then the floor is recommended.

2. It is much easier to elicit the Relaxation Response (RR) in the same place each day. Try reserving that place for your relaxation; you will find that you will start to relax simply by sitting there. Make sure that the phone is unplugged, the door is closed, and your pets are absent (pets are strangely attracted to a relaxed person!).

3. It is also easier to elicit the RR at the same time(s) each day. This helps make it a habit.

4. If you are eliciting the RR on your own (i.e. not with a tape), do not set a timer. Sit opposite a clock and when you think that the time is up, slowly get up. If the time is not up, simply close your eyes and go back to what you were focusing on.

5. It is quite normal for thoughts to come and go as you elicit the RR. Simply note that your mind has wandered, passively ignore the thoughts, and go back to what you were focusing on.

6. If you regularly exercise, try eliciting the RR immediately after you exercise; the sense of deep relaxation should come more easily.

7. Try not to elicit the RR either when you are very hungry or when you are full. Try having a glass of juice or a piece of fruit if you are hungry before sitting down. Wait a couple of hours after a full meal.

We generally advise eliciting the RR twice a day for 20 minutes each session. If you simply cannot fit in a session, try focusing on your breath for even five minutes. The only "bad RR" is one not done.

(Worksheet, courtesy of the Benson-Henry Institute for Mind Body Medicine, www.bensonhenryinstitute.org)

Focus Word or Phrase

The most universal methods of focusing your mind are linked to breathing, either by concentrating on your breathing itself or using it in conjunction with a focus word. Your focus word or mantra can be a word, phrase, or short prayer. "Mantra" means "the word that protects." When your mind is focused, you cannot dwell on negative, anxious thoughts.

A mantra has been a part of meditation and prayer in both Eastern and Western cultures for thousands of years. It is an anchor that helps you to quiet the self-talk chatter of your mind as you begin to meditate and pray.

Choosing your focus word is an important personal step. Tailor your focus word to your personal beliefs. This is often the best way to get maximum benefit from the relaxation response.

If your focus word has special meaning, it will not only be more effective in meditation and prayer, but also you will likely become more deeply involved in practicing the relaxation response. The combination of the relaxation response with a personal belief system is sometimes called "the faith factor."

Some, however, prefer their focus word to have no connection to a belief system and choose a more neutral word or phrase. It may be meaningless, without any emotion or intellectual associations. It is usually a soothing, pleasant sound that has no sharp or irritating characteristics. Regardless of the particular word or phrase chosen, it is a key to eliciting the relaxation response through meditation and prayer.

Keep the word or phrase short enough to coordinate easily with your breath. The list below offers a range of focus words or phrases from which to choose. Choose one that most appeals to you or create your own if you prefer.

(Worksheet, from *The Wellness Book: The Comprehensive Guide to Maintaining Health and Treating Stress-related Illness,*

44

courtesy of the Benson-Henry Institute for Mind Body Medicine, www.bensonhenryinstitute.org)

Common Focus Words or Phrases

General
*One   Peace   Calm   Let go   Relax   Light   Ocean   Oh well
Let it be   My time   Love Joy*

Christian
*God   Come, Lord   Lord, have mercy   Our Father
Our Father, who art in heaven   Jesus Saves
Lord Jesus Christ, Son of God, have mercy on me* (a *sinner*).
*Lord Jesus Christ, have mercy on me.   Hail Mary
The Lord is my shepherd   Abba ("Father")*

Jewish
*Sh'ma Yisroel ("Hear, o Israel") Echod ("One")
Shalom ("Peace") Hashem ("The Name")*

Eastern
*Om (the universal sound)   Hong-sau
Shantih ("Peace")   So-ham*

Aramaic
Maranatha ("Come, Lord")

Islamic
Allah

(Worksheet, from *The Wellness Book: The Comprehensive Guide to Maintaining Health and Treating Stress-related Illness*, courtesy of the Benson-Henry Institute for Mind Body Medicine, www.bensonhenryinstitute.org)

I do want to add a note of caution about selecting your mantra. Powerful mantras are often individualized, often have special meaning to the user. But they should be **spiritually uplifting**. Most people would say that is obvious, but experience teaches me otherwise. I once had a student who chose the following mantra: "Hate" on the in-breath, and "Kill" on the out-breath. Unfortunately, he practiced this mantra for several weeks before I learned what he was doing. He reported that practicing this mantra left his mind "agitated and unsettled."

Christian Centering Prayer

Introduction to Christian Centering Prayer

I was excited to discover and learn about a Christian contemplative spiritual tradition. I knew that Christian Centering Prayer would be more acceptable to the many Christians with whom I worked, and encourage them to practice contemplative meditation/prayer. Many Christians were uncomfortable learning about meditation/prayer unless it was presented in a Christian tradition.

Not Teaching Religion but God-realization I am not interested in teaching religion. What I want to teach is how to be closer to God, how to enter into the Kingdom of God! Each of us has this river of God's grace flowing beneath us. We need to dig a deep well to tap into this grace. If one is fortunate enough to have developed a heart connection to God during religious training in childhood, then that existing well should be dug deeper through meditation/prayer practice.

It makes no sense to change religions and start digging a brand new well. I am convinced that all religions, all meditation/prayer techniques, eventually bring the practitioner to the same place. "Truth is One; Paths are Many!" The challenge is to motivate the person to actually begin a meditation/prayer practice.

Father Thomas Keating is a founder of the Centering Prayer Movement and of Contemplative Outreach. (I am grateful for permission to use this material. For information about Contemplative Outreach, see www.contemplativeoutreach.org)

In *Open Mind, Open Heart,* Father Keating states, "There are all kinds of ways in which God speaks to us – through our thoughts or any one of our faculties. But keep in mind that God's first language is silence." (p. 57)

> The root of prayer is interior silence. We may think of prayer as thoughts or feelings expressed in words, but this is only one of its forms. ... Contemplative Prayer is not so much the absence of thoughts as detachment from them. It is the opening of mind and heart, body and emotions – our whole being – to God, the Ultimate Mystery, beyond words, thoughts, and emotions – beyond, in other words, the psychological content of the present moment. (p.14)

Father Thomas Keating explains that, through the regular practice of contemplative prayer, interior purification occurs. "This dynamism is a kind of divine psychotherapy, organically designed for each of us, to empty out our unconscious and free us from the obstacles to the free flow of grace in our minds, emotions, and bodies" (p. 93).

Through this divine psychotherapy, one moves from the "false self" to the "true self." Father Thomas Keating describes the "false self" and the "true self":

> **False Self** – the self developed in our own likeness rather than in the likeness of God; the self-image developed to cope with the emotional trauma of early childhood, which seeks happiness in satisfying the instinctual needs of survival/security, affection/esteem, and power/control, and which basis its self-worth on cultural or group identification.

> **True Self** – the image of God in which every human being is created; our participation in the divine life manifested in our uniqueness. (Keating, T. (1992). *Open*

mind, open heart: The contemplative dimension of the Gospel. New York, New York: Continuum. pp. 146-147.)

Proponents insist that Christian Centering Prayer is not mantra meditation, but in many ways it certainly looks like it.

One difference cited is that a mantra is loudly repeated, totally occupying the mind, while the sacred word is introduced gently, "as laying a feather on a piece of absorbent cotton." [Keating, T. (1995). *The method of centering prayer.* Butler, NJ: Contemplative Outreach. Used with permission.] I am not going to argue such distinctions, because I have great respect for both traditions.

And I urge you not to disregard Centering Prayer because you are not a Christian. Please always keep in mind, "Truth is One; Paths are many." If you read Father Thomas Keating's writings, it is obvious he has spent many hours in God-consciousness. Many points in Centering Prayer apply to all meditation techniques and are worth your time studying.

The Method of Christian Centering Prayer

The Guidelines

1. CHOOSE A SACRED WORD AS THE SYMBOL OF YOUR INTENTION TO CONSENT TO GOD'S PRESENCE AND ACTION WITHIN.

2. SITTING COMFORTABLY AND WITH EYES CLOSED, SETTLE BRIEFLY AND SILENTLY INTRODUCE THE SACRED WORD AS THE SYMBOL OF YOUR CONSENT TO GOD'S PRESENCE AND ACTION WITHIN.

3. WHEN YOU BECOME AWARE OF THOUGHTS, RETURN EVER-SO-GENTLY TO THE SACRED WORD.

4.   AT THE END OF THE PRAYER PERIOD, REMAIN IN SILENCE WITH EYES CLOSED FOR A COUPLE OF MINUTES.

Contemplative Prayer   Contemplative Prayer is the normal development of the grace of baptism and the regular practice of *Lectio Divina*. [*Lectio Divina* is the reading and listening to biblical texts and is the most ancient method of developing the friendship of Christ.] We may think of prayer as thoughts or feelings expressed in words, but this is only one expression.

Contemplative Prayer is the opening of mind and heart – our whole being – to God, the Ultimate Mystery, beyond thoughts, words, and emotions. We open our awareness to God whom we know by faith is within us, closer than breathing, closer than thinking, closer than choosing – closer than consciousness itself. Contemplative prayer is a process of interior purification leading, if we consent, to divine union.

The Method   Centering Prayer is a method designed to facilitate the development of contemplative prayer by preparing our faculties to cooperate with this gift

It is not meant to replace other kinds of prayer; it simply puts other kinds of prayer into a new and fuller perspective. During the time of prayer, we consent to God's presence and action within. At other times our attention moves outward to discover God's presence everywhere.

Explanation of the Guidelines

I. "Choose a sacred word as the symbol of your intention to consent to God's presence and action within." (cf. *Open Mind, Open Heart*, chap. 5)

1. The sacred word expresses our intention to be in God's presence and to yield to the divine action.

2. The sacred word should be chosen during a brief period of prayer asking the Holy Spirit to inspire us with one that is especially suitable to us.

a) Examples: Lord, Jesus, Father, Mother, Mary; or in other languages: Kyrie, Jesu, Jeshua, Abba, Mater, Maria.

b) Other possibilities: Love, Peace, Mercy, Silence, Stillness, Calm, Faith, Trust, Yes; or in other languages: Amor, Shalom, Amen.

3. Having chosen a sacred word, we do not change it during the prayer period, for that would be to start thinking again.

4. A simple inward gaze upon God may be more suitable for some persons than the sacred word. In this case, one consents to God's presence and action by turning inwardly to God as if gazing upon Him. The same guidelines apply to the sacred gaze as to the sacred word.

II. "Sitting comfortably and with eyes closed, settle briefly and silently introduce the sacred word as the symbol of your consent to God's presence and action within."

1. By "sitting comfortably" is meant relatively comfortably; not so comfortably that we encourage sleep, but sitting comfortably enough to avoid thinking about the discomfort of our bodies during the time of prayer.

2. Whatever sitting position we choose, we keep the back straight.

3. If we fall asleep, we continue the prayer for a few minutes upon awakening if we can spare the time.

4. Praying in this way after a main meal encourages drowsiness. Better to wait an hour at least before Centering Prayer. Praying in this way just before retiring may disturb one's sleep pattern.

5. We close our eyes to let go of what is going on around and within us.

6. We introduce the sacred word inwardly and as gently as laying a feather on a piece of absorbent cotton.

III. "When you become aware of thoughts, return ever-so-gently to the sacred word."

1. "Thoughts" is an umbrella term for every perception including sense perceptions, feelings, images, memories, reflections, and commentaries.

2. Thoughts are a normal part of Centering Prayer.

3. By "returning ever-so-gently to the sacred word", a minimum of effort is indicated. This is the only activity we initiate during the time of Centering Prayer.

4. During the course of our prayer, the sacred word may become vague or even disappear.

IV. "At the end of prayer period, remain in silence with eyes closed for a couple of minutes."
The additional 2 or 3 minutes give the psyche time to readjust to the external senses and enable us to bring the atmosphere of silence into daily life.

Some Practical Points

1. The minimum time for this prayer is 20 minutes. Two periods are recommended each day, one first thing in the morning, and one in the afternoon or early evening.

2. The end of the prayer period can be indicated by a timer, provided it does not have an audible tick or loud sound when goes off.

3. The principal effects of Centering Prayer are experienced in daily life, not in the period of Centering Prayer itself.

4. Physical Symptoms:

a. We may notice slight pains, itches, or twitches in various parts of the body or a generalized restlessness. These are usually due to the untying of emotional knots in the body.

b. We may also notice heaviness or lightness in the extremities. This is usually due to a deep level of spiritual attentiveness.

c. In either case, we pay no attention, or we allow the mind to rest briefly in the sensation, and then return to the sacred word.

5. *Lectio Divina* provides the conceptual background for the development of Centering Prayer.

6. A support group praying and sharing together once a week helps maintain one's commitment to the prayer.

Points for Further Development

1. During the prayer period various kinds of thoughts may be distinguished. (cf. *Open mind, open heart*, chap. 6-10):

a. Ordinary wanderings of the imagination or memory.
b. Thoughts that give rise to attractions or aversions.
c. Insights and psychological breakthroughs.
d. Self-reflections such as, "How am I doing?" or, "This peace is just great!"
e. Thoughts that arise from the unloading of the unconscious.

2. During this prayer we avoid analyzing our experience, harboring expectations or aiming at some specific goal such as:

a. Repeating the sacred word continuously.
b. Having no thoughts.
c. Making the mind a blank.
d. Feeling peaceful or consoled.
e. Achieving a spiritual experience.

3. What Centering Prayer is:

a. It is at the same time a relationship with God and a discipline to foster that relationship.
b. It is an exercise of faith, hope, and love.
c. It is a movement beyond conversation with Christ to communion.
d. It habituates us to the language of God which is silence.

Adapted from Keating, T. (1995). *The method of centering prayer.* Butler, NJ: Contemplative Outreach. Used with permission.

Don't judge centering prayer on the basis of how many thoughts come or how much peace you enjoy. The only way to judge this prayer is by its long-range fruits: whether in daily life you enjoy greater peace, humility and charity. Having come to deep interior silence, you begin to relate to others beyond the superficial aspects of social status, race, nationality, religion, and personal characteristics. (Keating, T. (1995). *Open mind, open heart.* p. 114.)

Inner Sound and Light Meditation

Caffeine

The Bible states, "In the beginning was the Word, and the Word was with God, and the Word was God" (John 1:1, KJV). In yoga, the Word is *Om* (Aum). The sound of *Om* is primordial, omnipresent, omnipotent, and omniscient.

I realize that most people do not consider caffeine to be a powerful drug or a problem. But my caffeine use kept me from hearing the inner sound of God, the sound of *Om*, which permeates the universe.

I discovered this quite by accident. During my seven- and ten-day silent retreats, caffeine was not available and, by the end of the retreat, I was clean, cleared of its effects. Over the years I learned that, when I was not on caffeine, I could hear the sound of *Om*, the sound of God. When I was on caffeine, I could not.

I also found listening to *Om*, the sound of God, to be very comforting, and strengthening. So I had a choice to make. On one hand I could have caffeine; on the other hand I could have the sound of God. It was an easy choice to make.

I chose God!

> The evidential aspect of God is *Om.* [Sustained] meditation on *Om* culminates in knowledge of it and God-realization. – Yoga-sutra 1:27&29

Technique of Primordial Sound and Light Contemplation

I realize that you may wish to learn to listen to your inner sound, the sound of God, and see the inner light. Roy Eugene Davis, in his book, *Seven Lessons in Conscious Living* (CSA Press, 2013, pp. 56-58) outlines the steps to follow to listen to your inner sound and see the inner light:

- Use your usual technique to meditate to the stage of tranquil, thought-free awareness.
- With your awareness at the spiritual eye center and higher brain, listen inside your ears and in your head until you discern a subtle sound. When a sound is heard, endeavor to hear a subtle sound behind it. Continue until you hear a sound that does not change.
- Blend your awareness with that sound. Merge in it.
- If you perceive inner light, blend your awareness with it as you merge your awareness with the sound.
- Gently inquire into the source of sound and light.
- Continue to meditate until you perceive that you are one with *Om* or until, having transcended it, you experience pure awareness of Being or a perception of oneness or wholeness.

The first sounds you hear may be those which occur naturally in the inner ear. As your attention becomes more internalized, you may discern the various subtle sound-frequencies of the vital centers (chakras) in the spinal pathway.

Eventually, when you hear a constant sound, use it as a mantra. Hear and perceive it in and outside of your head. Consider it as an aspect of *Om* which pervades your body and the universe. Expand and merge your awareness with it. If you perceive inner light, merge your awareness in it and *Om*.

Some meditators perceive a golden light, or a field of dark blue with a golden halo. They may also see a brilliant white light in the blue field. The teachers of this kriya yoga tradition declare golden light to be the radiance of *Om*; the dark blue to be the radiance of Consciousness-Intelligence that pervades the universe; and the brilliant white light to be the radiance of Consciousness itself.

If inner light is not easily perceived while contemplating *Om*, do not despair. Light perception, while of interest, is not as important as the clarification of awareness and the emergence of Self- and God-knowledge. Light perception is more likely when the waves of thoughts and emotions are pacified and remain dormant.

Any subjective perception of mental imagery (of people or other kinds of images) should be disregarded. The purpose of meditation practice is to transcend such phenomena. They are indications that desires, restlessness, and tendencies arising from the subconscious level of the mind are still influential. Be alert and attentive when meditating, yet patient as you learn by practice to acquire control of your attention and your states of awareness.

> I am dyed in the color of the Lord's name [*Om*],
> In a hue that can never fade;
> There is no color in the world
> That can be compared to the Lord's name. (Kabir)

(Above Section Used with Permission)

UNINTERRUPTED AWARENESS

To develop uninterrupted awareness, most people must practice meditation/prayer consistently for a long period of time with great effort. For many years after I learned the Serenity Meditation and later vipassana, mantra, and Kriya Pranayama meditations, I faithfully practiced meditation and reaped many positive benefits from my practice.

However, it was not until I participated in my first Integral Yoga® class series and added a regular Yoga practice to my spiritual practices did my meditations immediately deepen to levels I had never previously experienced. In fact, the impact was so profound that I resolved to become a Yoga teacher and share this jewel of Yoga with others.

After all, I had discovered meditation as the key to entering the Kingdom of God within. Anything that deepened meditation practice was precious knowledge and demanded to be shared with all!

From the many yoga training programs available, I chose Integral Yoga® teacher training. Every Integral Yoga® class included meditation. I knew that some yoga teacher training programs dealt only superficially with meditation. Some ignored meditation altogether.

In the West, yoga has been de-spiritualized! Meditation, the heart of yoga, is the most important part and food for the spirit. It is often ignored. Only the postures, the *asanas,* food for the body, are emphasized.

Integral Yoga® feeds both the body and the soul. In every class, it integrates four major practices – *asanas* (postures), *pranayama* (breath control), *yoga nidra* (deep relaxation), and meditation.

I wanted to learn a balanced approach, an approach that included the jewel of meditation. As part of my Integral Yoga® training, I learned yoga philosophy and began to incorporate these teachings into my daily life. I include them here and recommend that you (the reader) study them and adopt them into your life, consistent with your own spiritual beliefs.

Once again let me emphasize that I am not interested in teaching religion. My goal in this book is to teach spiritual practices that you can incorporate into your own personal philosophy.

Yoga Philosophy

From Satchidananda Ashram

Eastern philosophy and psychology teach that the human psyche is veiled with many layers of ignorance that obscure our ability to see the Divine within us. However, at the deepest levels of being, we search for ways to re-establish our connection with our spiritual nature. For this reason, according to Eastern wisdom, we take on a human form.

Our activities while on Earth help us to work through the layers of ignorance, one by one. Finally, after much time and experience, we come to understand the true meaning of Self. In the moment of Self-realization, the ego is made free – free from the weight of all its illusions and free to reach its eternal destiny.

In this context, the body is a temple and also an instrument that allows us to experience life. A musician regularly tunes his instrument to improve its performance, cleaning and preparing it in a series of movements that look to us like little rituals. Similarly, taking care of the body is a ritualistic tuning by which we grow and perfect ourselves.

Regular exercise can do more than establish good health and a youthful appearance. When practiced with a devotional attitude, as a form of worship, physical activity keeps us in tune with life's purpose. Worship means devotion to something we love, admire, and respect. By exercising the body we show respect for the physical instrument that houses the spirit.

We should never begin a routine of physical exercise because we want to be superior to others in strength, or beauty. Sometimes, the more we become accomplished in life's activities, the more our ego is inflated. We see ourselves as masterful and, therefore, better than others.

There are two motivations for any activity in life. We can improve ourselves at the expense of others and obstruct our own growth, or we can improve our surroundings, help others to improve and, thereby, expand ourselves.

As we develop more physical and mental balance and strength we participate more fully in creating healthier societies and environments and, finally, a healthier planet. Of all forms of movement, Yoga exercise ranks at the top because its purpose is to create balance in the body and mind.

Unfortunately, some people associate Yoga with mystical religions and cults. This misinterpretation of the science and philosophy of Yoga has discouraged many seekers of health who might, otherwise, benefit from this ancient practice.

We have found no other system that is as comprehensive and contributes as much to mind-body wellness as Yoga. The word "Yoga" means union. All exercises in Yoga, both physical and mental, are designed to unite the body with the mind and the individual self with the Self of all.

The physical exercises in Yoga, balance, stretch, tone, and strengthen the body in such a way that the nervous system and the mind can also be balanced and strengthened. Yoga exercises are based upon the premise that our mental and physical bodies work in synergy and that wherever there is synergistic harmony, there is health.

In Yoga there is no winning, or losing, and no competition with self, or others. Instead, all of our physical and mental activities become means to achieving the ultimate goal in life, the realization of our Divine Nature.

(Above Section Used with Permission)

Integral Yoga®

From Satchidananda Ashram

Integral Yoga is the synthesis of the various branches of Yoga. It is a scientific system for the harmonious development of every aspect of the individual. The following are some of its different branches.

HATHA YOGA: Predominantly concerned with the physical development, through asanas (postures), pranayama (breath control), deep relaxation, etc.

RAJA YOGA: Predominantly concerned with the control of the mind, through ethical perfection and regular practice of concentration and meditation.

BHAKTI YOGA: The path of devotion. By constant love, thought, and service of the Divine (either as God, a Divine Incarnation, or the spiritual teacher), the individual transcends his/her limited personality and attains Cosmic Consciousness. The path of Bhakti can be practiced by everyone. All that is needed is faith and constant remembrance of God.

JAPA YOGA: Japa Yoga is a part of Raja Yoga. Japa means repetition of a mantram. A mantram is a sound structure of one or more syllables which represents a particular aspect of the Divine Vibration. Concentrated mental repetition of the mantram produces vibrations within the individual's entire system which are in tune with the Divine Vibration.

KARMA YOGA: The path of action. By surrendering his/her individual will to the Cosmic Will, the practitioner becomes attuned to the freedom of his own actionless Self.

JNANA YOGA: The intellectual approach. Through the knowledge of what really exists, that is, what is not changeable, the Jnani (one who engages in the Path of Wisdom) realizes Oneness with the entire Universe.

(Above Section Used with Permission)

It is useful to remember that all these paths to God are equally valid; all lead to the same goal. "Paths are many; truth is one." Some personalities are better suited to a particular path. For example, I am drawn to Bhakti Yoga, the path of devotion.

Raja Yoga: The Yoga of Meditation

From Satchidananda Ashram

As a lamp placed in a windless spot does not flicker – to such is compared the Yogi of controlled mind, practicing Yoga in the Self (or absorbed in the Yoga of the Self).
Bhagavad Gita, 6.19

In the study of Raja Yoga no faith or belief is necessary. Believe nothing until you find it out for yourself – that is what it teaches us. Truth requires no prop to make it stand.
Raja Yoga, Swami Vivekananda

Yoga means union. Union with the Divine is the ultimate aim. Raja Yoga is the royal path, for Raja means king. Raja Yoga deals with the mind directly and is, therefore, called the Kingly Yoga. It is also called Ashtanga Yoga, ashtanga meaning eight-fold. There are eight steps in the ladder of Raja Yoga. These are:

1.   YAMA (Restraints)

a. Ahimsa (harmlessness, non-violence)
b. Satya (truthfulness)
c. Brahmacharya (continence)
d. Asteya (non-stealing, non-covetousness)
e. Asparigraha (non-hoarding)

2.   NIYAMA (Observances)

a. Saucha (purity, internal and external)
b. Santosha (contentment)
c. Tapas (austerity)
d. Svadhyaya (spiritual study)
e. Ishwarapranidhana (self-surrender to the Lord)

3.   ASANA (Physical posture)

4.   PRANAYAMA (Breath regulation)

5.   PRATYAHARA (Withdrawing of the senses)

6.   DHARANA (Concentration on one point)

7.   DHYANA (Meditation, the steady flow of thought upon one point)

8.   SAMADHI (Absorption, subject and object become one)

(Above Section Used with Permission)

Note that the *Yamas* (Restraints) and *Niyamas* (Obervances) form the foundation practices. That is, success is unlikely without living the *Yamas* and *Niyamas*. *Samadhi,* union with God, is improbable. If you want to develop uninterrupted awareness, you must live a moral life. For example, if you lie, steal, cheat, kill, and engage in sexual misconduct, etc., it is highly unlikely that your mind will be calm and peaceful enough to experience uninterrupted awareness.

In addition to living a moral life, for most folks to achieve "uninterrupted awareness" requires a great deal of practice. The mind is like a wild, drunken monkey trapped in a cage and stung by a scorpion. To tame the mind requires a lot of loving patience.

I have now been meditating for over thirty years, and there still are days that I experience "monkey mind." When I remind myself that God loves me just as I am, I am encouraged and continue my practice.

I am also comforted by what Swami Satchidananda says about meditation:

> Meditation is to calm the mind, to bring the mind together. If you are already restful and peaceful, why do you need meditation? Meditation is a sort of medication. So, if you feel any disturbance in the mind, try to calm down the mind by practicing meditation. Don't get disappointed if you can't meditate right away. Nothing is achieved overnight. When did you learn to walk or run? From the beginning? No. When you were a baby, you couldn't even stand up, you couldn't even crawl. Then you gradually learned to crawl, and walk, and run. Meditation is also like that. (Used with Permission)

In Conclusion

Meditation is a relaxed, focused, uninterrupted awareness. This short book outlines how you may develop and deepen your own personal meditation/prayer practice.

As my meditations deepened, I experienced a great deal of fear. I had to learn to "let go and let God." After I was born, I spent many years building, developing, my ego. But success in meditation required that I let it go and merge in the infinite. It was my path to Self- and God-realization.

It is ironic that this struggle exists for most of us. You may experience it also. I discovered, and you may too, that there is no need for fear. This struggle is a paradox. The ego, the bubble, can become part of the sea, and yet will still be the bubble. The individual ego can survive, though **transformed**!

Remember, meditation/prayer is not about getting high; it is not about bliss. Often, I have to remind myself not to be too satisfied resting in Bliss-consciousness. As much as I love it, that is not my goal.

Rather, my goal is Self- and God-realization. I once asked Roy Eugene Davis, my guru (teacher), how I could become fully Self- and God-realized. He laughed and said that he wished he could tell me but he could not. Then he gently explained that is a path I have to discover for myself.

You, too, will have to discover the path for yourself. I wish you God speed on this very special journey and stand ready to assist you in any way that I can.

Made in the USA
Columbia, SC
13 October 2023

23954046R00041